To
for Comfort

by Linda Lott

illustrated by Kathryn Adams

MODERN CURRICULUM PRESS

Pearson Learning Group

Chapter 1 • Good News, Bad News

The note was on the refrigerator when Jerry came down to breakfast. It said, "Family Meeting Tonight." Jerry opened the refrigerator and poured glasses of juice for himself and his little brother, Jimmy. He wasn't worried about the meeting. After all, a family meeting didn't usually mean trouble. Sometimes family meetings were even fun. Maybe it was time to plan a vacation. Or maybe Mom and Dad were going to buy something big, like a computer. When a big decision needed to be made, Mom and Dad always talked it over with the boys. The boys were encouraged to give their opinions. And if money was involved, Jerry and Jimmy had to tell how they would contribute.

Of course, sometimes family meetings were about rules. But even those meetings weren't too bad. There was at least a fifty-fifty chance that Jimmy would be the one who was in trouble. Jerry paused, holding the juice bottle in midair. He couldn't think of any rules he had broken lately. If anybody was in trouble this time, Jerry thought with a grin, it would be Jimmy.

Just then Jimmy appeared, stretching and yawning. He was dressed for school, but he was still carrying the beat-up monster toy he slept with every night.

"Hey," Jerry teased, "you're not going to take that doll to school, are you?"

Jimmy was used to his big brother's teasing. "It's not a doll," Jimmy stated, unperturbed. "It's Monster. And it just so happens that I *am* taking him to school. I'm going to read a story to him during free reading time."

"Can you read this?" Jerry said, pointing to the memo on the refrigerator. "You must be in big trouble. Maybe Mom and Dad have decided it's time for you to get rid of all those stuffed animals you keep in your room."

Jimmy slowly read the note on the refrigerator. " 'Family Meeting Tonight.' I'll be there. I'm not worried. And it's my room. I can keep anything I want in there."

"We'll see," Jerry teased. He finished his breakfast, carried his dishes to the dishwasher, and left to get ready for school.

That evening after dinner the family assembled in the living room. Mom and Dad looked pretty serious. Jerry and Jimmy, sitting together on the couch, both squirmed a little. Maybe they had broken some rule, they thought.

Then Mom smiled. "We have some news," she said. "There are going to be a few changes around here. We think you'll be delighted with them, but we also think you need to know precisely what to expect."

"Grandpa's coming to live with us," Dad said.

"Hurray!" Jimmy shouted. The boys loved spending time with their grandfather.

But Jerry was thoughtful. "Why is Grandpa leaving his house?" he asked quietly. "Is something wrong with Grandpa?"

"Grandpa's fine," Mom reassured Jerry. "But his doctor has discovered some problems with his eyesight, and we think Grandpa shouldn't live alone anymore. If blindness is in his future, we want him to get used to living in this house now."

"I don't care why Grandpa's coming," Jimmy said. "I'm just glad he is. He can stay with me in my room. I'll let him have the top bunk. He even likes my stuffed animals," Jimmy added, with a smug look at his brother.

"I'm glad you're happy about living with Grandpa," Mom said gently. "And I know Grandpa will be happy about spending more time with you boys. But I think he would be more comfortable with a room of his own."

Suddenly Jerry was beginning to see where the conversation was going. He glanced at Jimmy, but Jimmy didn't seem to have a clue yet.

"But we don't have an extra room," Jerry said. "We could give him the living room. But then where would we watch TV and play games? Maybe we could turn the garage into a room for Grandpa."

Dad smiled. "Your ideas have merit," he said. "But I don't think they're just right for Grandpa. Mom and I think the best idea is to give Grandpa Jimmy's downstairs bedroom. Jimmy, you can share Jerry's room."

Jimmy and Jerry looked at each other. Grandpa's moving in was good news. But here was the bad news. For brothers, they got along pretty well. But maybe that was because they had their own spaces. They both liked having their own rooms. And they each had very different ideas about what was important in a bedroom.

"We know sharing a room won't be easy," Mom said quickly. "But we trust you boys to work things out. Be creative! We can't afford to spend any money, but we'll help you as much as we can."

That night, neither boy went to sleep right away. Both boys spent some time looking around their own rooms . . . and enjoying them!

Jerry liked open space. He didn't want lots of junk in his room. He had a grown-up looking plaid spread and one sports poster. His computer was on his desk, and a bookshelf held his favorite books, a few model cars, and computer disks. Everything he needed and wanted was right there. And everything was organized and easy to find.

Jimmy had everything he wanted in his room too. But Jimmy's idea of cozy was Jerry's idea of cluttered. Jimmy's collection of stuffed animals was his favorite thing. And no matter what Jerry said, Jimmy refused to call them dolls. He had stuffed monsters and fierce tigers and bears. They were sitting on the floor, on shelves, and on the bed. His toy chest overflowed too. Jimmy knew six-year-olds needed things like blocks. He also needed games to play with his friends when they came to visit.

Jimmy secretly thought his big brother was very cool, but Jimmy was not sure there were any advantages in sharing a room with him. What if Jerry wanted to sleep without a nightlight?

"I probably won't ever be able to sleep again," Jimmy said to himself. "At least not until I'm grown up."

Chapter 2 • Brotherly Love

On Saturday morning, Dad usually slept late. But on the morning after the family meeting, he was up bright and early. From their rooms, Jerry and Jimmy could hear Dad bustling around as he got dressed and made breakfast. He even whistled as he worked.

On this last morning in their separate rooms, both boys squeezed their eyes shut, determined to stay in bed as long as possible. Finally, Dad shouted, "Rise and shine!" Knowing they could no longer avoid facing this day, Jerry and Jimmy got up and made their way to the kitchen.

"This is the big day, boys," Dad said cheerfully. "Moving day!"

"Right," Jerry and Jimmy answered glumly.

Almost before they realized it, the whole family was hard at work. Jerry moved his desk and his poster over beside his bed and emptied out his extra closet. Mom and Jimmy loaded Jimmy's toys into cartons. And Dad took apart Jimmy's bunk bed so it would be easy to move. Then the entire family cooperated to carry Jimmy's belongings upstairs. By late afternoon, everything was in place.

Later, in their shared room, the boys got ready for bed silently. Jimmy walked over to turn on his nightlight.

"I can't sleep with a light on," Jerry grumbled.

For the first time all day, Jimmy's lower lip started to tremble. He clutched Monster for moral support. "But I can't sleep in the dark," he wailed. "I'm afraid of the dark."

Jerry glanced at his little brother's eyes that were brimming with tears. "It must be tough to lose your room," he said. "At least I still have mine, even if it's different. And upstairs must seem awfully far away from Mom and Dad when you're a little kid."

"Okay," Jerry said gruffly. "I guess I can learn to live with a little light."

Jimmy grinned and curled up in his bed with Monster. "Thanks, Jerry," he said as he closed his eyes.

But Jerry didn't go to sleep quite so easily. As his eyes adjusted to the dim nightlight, he surveyed the damage for the first time. His neat, organized, uncluttered room looked like the aftermath of a tornado at the zoo. On every surface was a stuffed animal or two. More toys were lined up along the floor and spilling out of the toy chest. For the first time, Jerry noticed that Jimmy had even set a stuffed tiger right on the computer.

Jerry shut his eyes tight to block out the sight. He pulled the covers over his head.

The room looked even worse to Jerry in the bright morning sunlight. He hurried to get downstairs as quickly as possible. All morning, he avoided going up to his room. In the afternoon, he hopped on his bike and left for his soccer game long before he really had to.

But by the time Jerry and his friend Karl came home from the game, Jerry had forgotten all about his new roommate.

"How'd it go?" Dad called from the living room.

"Great! We won!" Jerry replied.

"And Jerry scored the winning goal!" added Karl.

"Wonderful," said Mom. "Why don't you two boys grab a snack. There are some apples in the bowl on the kitchen table."

Jerry and Karl raced to the kitchen to get the apples. Then they bounded upstairs to Jerry's room to rehash the game as usual. In the excitement, Jerry had forgotten all about his new roommate. But a moment later, as Karl stopped short at the door and Jerry bumped into him, it all came back. Jimmy was nowhere in sight, but he'd certainly spent the afternoon in the room. Toys that had been in the box were now scattered on the floor. And, worst of all, Jerry's own bed was covered with stuffed animals.

"Hey," Karl laughed. "I didn't know your ambitions included being a stuffed animal collector. Very cute!"

Jerry glared at Karl. "What do you know about my ambitions?" asked Jerry. But Karl kept laughing. Pretty soon Jerry managed to grin too. But he had a sick feeling in the pit of his stomach. Nothing would ever be the same. Quickly, he calculated the number of years left before he could leave home for college.

College, he concluded, was a long time away.

That night, after dinner, Jerry stopped Jimmy in the hallway.

"I'm calling a brothers' meeting," Jerry announced.

"A brothers' meeting?" Jimmy repeated. "I never heard of a brothers' meeting."

"It's pretty much like a family meeting," said Jerry, "but without Mom and Dad."

"I don't know if we should have a meeting without Mom and Dad," Jimmy said skeptically.

"Maybe not usually," answered Jerry, "but this time we have to. We have a problem, and Mom and Dad are counting on us to work it out by ourselves."

Jimmy was puzzled. "A problem?" he said. But he followed his big brother up the stairs obediently.

In the living room, Mom and Dad heard the boys clomping up the stairs together.

"I think sharing a room has already made the boys closer," Mom said happily.

Dad smiled at Mom. "It does kind of warm your heart to see them going off to their room together, doesn't it. They must have found out that there are some advantages to sharing a room."

In their room, Jerry swept a pile of stuffed animals off his bed and sat down. Jimmy sat on his own bed and pulled his toys closer.

"What did you mean when you said we have a problem?" Jimmy asked.

"Look around," answered Jerry. "Your toys are the problem. You still have every toy you ever got. They're everywhere!"

Jimmy was indignant. "My toys are *not* a problem," he protested. "They're very nice toys. I take very good care of them so they last a long time, and I like every single one. This room looked empty until I put my toys around. And you're lucky I'm willing to share them. All little brothers aren't as nice to their big brothers as I am!"

"You're a very nice little brother," Jerry responded patiently, "and your toys are nice too. For someone your age! I'm too old to play with your toys. I was embarrassed when Karl saw them all over my room."

"It's my room too!" Jimmy declared. "And I'm not getting rid of a single one!"

"I'm not asking you to get rid of them, Jimmy. I have another idea. I think it will make us both happy."

Jerry pulled a roll of masking tape from his pocket.

"What's that for?" Jimmy asked.

"It's part of my plan. I'll divide the room down the middle and mark the dividing line with this tape. I'll stay on my side of the line. You—and all your stuff—have to stay on your side of the line."

"But I have more stuff than you do!" Jimmy protested. "I'll never fit it all in."

"That's tough," Jerry replied. "Fair is fair. I said I'd share my room with you. I never said I'd give you my half too."

Jimmy watched suspiciously as Jerry used the tape to divide the room.

"Are you sure that's the middle?" he asked.

"I'm sure," Jerry replied. "And anything on this side of the line is my personal space. So start moving all your stuff over to your own side."

Reluctantly, Jimmy got off the bed. As he slowly began picking up his toys and moving them over the line, Jerry went to work on the second part of his project. He took a large sheet of cardboard from his desk and wrote "Keep Out" in big letters. Then he held up his new sign.

"Can you read this?" Jerry asked sternly.

"It says 'keep out,'" Jimmy replied, glaring at the sign. "And you keep out of my side too!"

The next morning, Jerry was surprised to wake up to see a big smile on Jimmy's face.

"Good morning," said Jerry. "I guess you've decided my plan is a good one after all."

"Fair's fair," Jimmy answered. "As Dad would say, your plan has merit."

But when Jerry began to cross through Jimmy's side of the room to get to the closet, his little brother jumped off the bed and blocked his way.

"Keep out!" he said.

"But I have to get dressed! My clothes are in the closet."

"Too bad," said Jimmy with an angelic smile. "The closet is on my side of the room."

Jerry thought for a minute. Then he said, "Fine. The clothes I wore yesterday are on my chair so I can wear them to school. But you won't even get to school! The door's on my side."

Defeated, Jimmy gave Jerry a dirty look. "OK," he said. "You win. Give me the tape. I'll mark a path between the closet and the door. You can come on my side, and I can go on your side. But we have to stay on the path."

"It's a deal," Jerry said angrily. Then he dressed and stomped down the stairs. At breakfast, neither brother spoke to the other.

As Jerry hurried home from school that afternoon, his little brother was the furthest thing from his mind. He was too busy worrying about the big social studies test that was coming up. Social studies was Jerry's hardest subject, and his social studies teacher was really strict. With all his little brother problems, Jerry had been too busy and too stressed even to think about the test. As Jerry walked in the front door, he went over his schedule in his mind. Jerry knew he'd have to study hard until bedtime.

Jerry said hi to Mom, grabbed a snack, and then raced up to his room to study. But at the top of the steps, he heard a racket coming from his room. He stopped at the door and looked in. Jimmy and two of his friends were playing some kind of wild, loud first-grade game on Jimmy's side of the room.

Jerry burst through the door. He tossed his books on his desk, and his notes spilled all over the floor.

"Beat it," he shouted. "I have an important test to study for."

Jimmy's friends stopped playing immediately. They looked at Jerry fearfully. But Jimmy glared at Jerry.

"Hey," he said, "you're not being fair. I invited my friends here to play. And we're on my side of the room."

"Well, the noise you're making is in the whole room. So go away!"

"No, you go away," Jimmy said crossly. "This is my room too. And my friends and I need our privacy!"

Jerry didn't have time to argue, so he gathered up his books and his notes that were all over the floor. His face was red with anger as he stalked off to find a quiet place to study for his test.

As his big brother left, Jimmy made a face at the door.

Just before bedtime, Jerry called another brothers' meeting. This time Jimmy knew what to expect.

"You're gonna make some more rules and regulations, aren't you?" he scowled. "And that means there'll be one more thing I can't do in my own room."

Jimmy crossed his arms and glared at Jerry.

"I'm just trying to make this work out," Jerry explained patiently. "Grandpa's coming. We can't change that. We're stuck together in this room. Those are circumstances we can't change."

Jerry took out another sheet of cardboard. Across the top he wrote "Schedule."

"You were right when you said you need privacy. I need privacy too. So here's what we'll do. We'll divide our time the way we divided our space. From the time you get home from school until I get home, the room is yours. Then I get the room until dinner time. After dinner, you get the room for an hour. Then I get the room until it's time for you to get ready for bed. I'm writing this down so there won't be any mistakes."

"I just hope you don't forget anything when you leave," Jimmy grumped, "because you won't get in at all when it's my turn for the room."

Jimmy slammed doors and drawers and stamped his feet angrily as he got ready for bed. Then he turned on his nightlight, and threw himself into bed. He turned his back to Jerry without saying goodnight.

Jerry got ready for bed thoughtfully. He couldn't sleep. Even though he sometimes got mad at his little brother, he knew that, as brothers go, Jimmy wasn't so bad. And until now they had gotten along pretty well. This room thing was ruining everything. Maybe it would be better if Grandpa weren't moving in with them.

Then Jerry closed his eyes and tried to imagine how blindness felt. He realized that Grandpa really needed his family. He really was glad Grandpa was coming to stay.

Jerry tossed and turned. The whole situation was a big problem, and Jerry had tried every solution he could think of to solve it. Nothing had helped. He and his brother, he decided, were going to grow up to be enemies, not friends as they had been. And there was nothing Jerry could do about it.

Chapter 3 • Three Heads Are Better Than Two

Once a week, Mom usually worked late. On those days, Jerry and Jimmy were in the habit of walking over to Grandpa's apartment to have dinner with him. Usually they had fun on the way. They laughed and talked. Sometimes they raced, and Jerry let Jimmy win. In the winter, the boys tossed snowballs at each other. But today was definitely different.

Jimmy marched down the sidewalk a few steps ahead of Jerry. Jerry sauntered behind with his hands in his pockets. Just before they reached Grandpa's door, Jerry called to Jimmy.

"Listen," he said, "just for today we have to act as if everything's OK. We can't let Grandpa see that we're fighting. He might guess what we're fighting about. If he knows we're fighting about sharing a room, he'll think it's his fault. Grandpa can't help having to come live with us, and we can't hurt his feelings."

Jimmy knew Jerry was right.

As the boys burst through the door, they both plastered big, fake smiles on their faces. But even though they tried hard to pretend that everything was normal, they couldn't fool Grandpa. After only a few minutes, Grandpa sensed that something was wrong.

"You boys don't seem to be getting along very well today," Grandpa observed. "We usually have so much fun together."

"No," Jerry assured Grandpa. "Everything's fine. I guess I'm just worried about the big test I had this week."

"Really?" Grandpa asked. "There's one thing we haven't talked about. I know your Mom and Dad told you I'll be coming to live with you. Are you worried? You don't need to worry, because I'm not. I'll get along just fine. There will be lots of advantages to living in the same house with you boys."

"Right!" both boys shouted out at once. "We want you to live with us. It'll be great to get to see you every day."

"Even so," Grandpa counseled, "changes are hard. I know you boys are sharing a room now. Things must feel pretty different."

Both boys looked down at the floor.

Jimmy couldn't contain himself any longer. He dashed over and sat on Grandpa's lap.

"Grandpa," he sobbed, "I thought it would be fun to move in with my big brother. But it's not. Everything is all squashed together, and Jerry's made up all kinds of rules. We don't have any fun together. We're always fighting."

For just a moment, Jerry regretted that he was too old to sit on Grandpa's lap. Miserably, he mumbled, "It's not that we don't want you to live with us. We do. We just have to get used to sharing a room."

"What problems are you having?" Grandpa inquired.

"Jimmy's got so much stuff," Jerry said. "His toys are all over everything."

"And Jerry doesn't like to sleep with the light on," Jimmy blurted. "I know one of these days he'll make a rule about that."

"And we both need privacy," the boys concluded jointly.

"Mom and Dad said we should work things out ourselves," Jerry added. "And I've tried everything I can think of. But I just can't seem to solve our problem."

"Another thing your mom and dad say is 'Two heads are better than one.' If that's so, then three heads should be even better than two. Maybe we could come up with a way for all of us to have our own rooms."

"Good idea," smiled Jimmy. "We could build another room onto the house. We could save money for it ourselves. Jerry could get a paper route, and I could walk Mrs. Armstrong's dog."

"Building a room is expensive," Jerry said scornfully. "By the time we save enough money for a new room, we'll be grown-ups with houses of our own."

"But that attic room of yours is pretty big," said Grandpa. "You don't need to add on a whole room. You just need a wall. And I may have a wall for you right here."

Grandpa led the boys on a tour of the house.

"When I move in with you," Grandpa said, "I'll need to get rid of most of my furniture. I'll bring my bedroom furniture, and my favorite chair, and your Grandmother's cabinet. That was her pride and joy. But the rest of the furniture will have to go, unless I can find a good use for it."

In the den, Grandpa pointed to the tall bookcases that lined the room.

"Bookcases!" Jerry exclaimed. "I never thought of them. We can use them to build a wall right down the middle of the room. Jimmy can have the shelf side for his toys. And we'll both have privacy!"

"See," said Grandpa. "You've solved your problem. And you used creativity instead of money."

The boys and Grandpa spent the next hour drawing a plan of their new room arrangement.

On moving day, Grandpa brought the furniture he would need for himself and the bookshelves for the boys. Dad, Jimmy, and Jerry carried the shelves up the stairs and lined them up in the middle of the room. Then the boys helped each other rearrange their furniture. Each boy had a window and a closet. They shared the door. Most importantly, each boy had his own space.

Just as they finished, Karl dropped over to visit. He looked at the two rooms with admiration.

"This arrangement is great," he said.

Jerry smiled happily from his neat, uncluttered room. And Jimmy smiled from the door of his toy-filled room.

"It is okay, isn't it?" Jerry said, looking around. "Having a little brother isn't so bad when you don't have to look at him all the time," he teased. "And there sure are advantages to having a grandfather living here in our own house–especially one who knows that three heads are better than two!"